Also by Bryan Wilton

Asatru Book of Days

Love and Hate in Asatru

The Collected Works on Asatru

Ansuz; Business, Life and The Valfathers Example

The Soldiers Edda

Understanding Asatru

Voluspa and Havamal Pocket Sized for the Troops

Asatru Awakening

An Asatru Life

Nobility

The Spiritual Journey of a Woman

Bryan & Stephanie Wilton

© 2017 Bryan D. Wilton. All rights reserved. No part of this work may be reproduced without the written consent of the owner 2015

ISBN: **1544203888**
ISBN-13: **978-1544203881**

Contents

Acknowledgements 6

Stephanie's Foreword 9

Preface 13

Chapter I 21

Chapter II 39

Chapter III 67

Chapter IV 81

Chapter V 105

Chapter VI 119

Acknowledgements

I have roughly a dozen or so books which I have started and gone no further with. The effort it takes to sit down a write a book, while it may seem easy, requires a good deal of thought and discipline. It also requires that my "heart" be in it. When I first approached My wife Stephanie and Mandy Dale of the AFA separately about writing a book concerning women, I was understandably met with some hesitation. So I reached out to two other women and I was willing to listen to their input. I would write and then I would share it and listen for feedback. My wife and I would argue about the direction of the book and the council of three would tell me to talk about this or talk about that. Together I think we have crafted a fantastic book which will serve the finest of ulterior motives. A book our daughter will always be able to treasure. What greater gift could I ever bestow upon my descendants. This book is for all of the women who have a need within our faith (or any faith for that matter) to find some kind of healing. So I would like to offer a special thanks to Stephanie Martin Wilton, my wife and the mother of our daughter Scarlett for working with me on this. Anyone who has ever seen this kind of work done between man and wife will understand the challenge of it. I would also like to thank Mandy Dale of the AFA for her unique southern input on what a woman really ought to be. Kristina Horacek LCSW for her input on the soundness of these ideas and their applicability to women. And finally; to Heather Clinkenbeard who has been a friend for several years, her courageous approach to tackling the problems of life have been an inspiration to more people than she realizes. Thank you all.

I would also like to thank my niece Adrianne Starr Miller for the use of her image on the cover of this book. And to my mom for taking the photograph. When I saw it I was struck by it in that the painting of the lady in red in the Augsberg city hall is supposed to be a representation of the Goddess Zisa, the partner of Tyr and who granted that city a victory against the Romans on the 28th of Sep.

        To Scarlett Anne Valentine Wilton

        Love Dad!

Stephanie's Foreword

Bryan Wilton has always found his peace and inner solace with writing. He has literally been penning his thoughts since childhood. As for myself I have found that like Bryan I too have journaled. My deepest feelings, my thoughts, my fears and well as my joy have found their voice through the music I have been able to play and write since I was a child performing for whatever church had asked to hear the prodigy of this little girl. Many times, I would visit a church and hear my music being played by someone else. I'm sure that somewhere they still are.

      Bryan and I happened into each others lives in July of 2010. Each of us going through a divorce and each of us searching for an inner peace and acceptance. Bryan had embarked on his alien and newfound spiritual path that I had told him one time was a "deal breaker". I dealt with my loss, affliction and emotional pain by becoming alternately numb or controlling and OCD like in my behaviors.

Ultimately in our deepest intimacy we created a special girl. Scarlett. (Surprise!) Our other beautiful children came along for the adventure. Darren, Heather, Alex and Jeff as well as little Shelbe', Kristin and Taylor.

These past two months have been deeply healing for me as a woman. I have found myself – yet I was always here. I have found my inner peace. In a deep, dark place I have found an extremely spiritual path to strength. I have discovered emotional clarity, physical endurance and above all, peace of mind. Something I cannot remember ever having.

Bryan and I have discovered each other and have found that we both have the same ideals (primarily) and core values. This is vital for a woman's heart. To be noticed and accepted as you are. To be beautiful as YOU – for the peaceful beauty that radiates from within to exude on the outside. Where others will feel your beauty. Through your smile and your creativity, Through passion, through music, through motherhood and beyond. But most importantly through embracing your inner peace.

I have very fond childhood memories of strong yet peacefully feminine women. Those women, years later, have helped me through my emotional and spiritual journey.

Find your inner peace. With this comes strength. Discover your inner beauty at your core and embrace the real *you*.

Stephanie Wilton

Mar 27 2017

Preface

In late 2016 I did an interview with the `Barbarian Lounge Podcast. During this interview the thought occurred to me and me immediately said "Given the state of things; how long do you think we have to get our stuff together." I was referring to the state of affairs within the Asatru/Odinist/Heathen community. With so many different ideas and reasons for a person to be just as loyal as they can to an idea, it has created a fantastic environment where anyone may enter the fray online and submit one of those contentious ideas which serves only to separate and confuse the community. It happens every single day. From the folks who want to denigrate the lore and the nine noble virtues to boost their own importance to people of very different faiths offering an uninvited outside opinion; the list of people who are interested in seeing the failure of this resurgence of the folk soul far outnumber those of us who wish to embrace it. And we have largely failed to sufficiently empower the unifying ideals which allowed the random tribes of Germania to resist the Roman Empire.

There is a reason for that. The very mindset of the heathen is at odds with the status of the world around him. He does not conform or fit in. He sees other folks going to work day in and day out, making money to pay off debt and wonders two things. Why can't I do that and why would I do that. Some few individuals, through sheer strength of will and what they consider to be holy, empower themselves to fall in line and behave like the rest of society. By all accounts they consider themselves to be successful. They have seemingly handled the obstacles of their own minds. Perseverance, self-reliance and industriousness are their hallmarks. Yet the breakthrough they have read about by lesser men and women eludes them. The dropout, never do well, geek who almost overnight and despite his social shortcomings surpasses the greatest dreams we may have entertained as a child is a mystery to us, yet somehow there may be an inkling of the truth of the matter in their own minds, the fears we have been taught may well be robbing us of our future. Money flows to these tech wizards almost as if by magic. While we may be forced to continue working jobs we hate. Doing our best to try and live for the weekend when we might be able to cut free and enjoy a day or two with our families. If we can afford it. It is the norm, but it is not the norm we were bred for.

The modern-day diagnosis of mental illness typically corresponds with the individual who cannot or will not fit the mold of literally millions of men and women around the world. We have allowed the world to be changed in such a manner that we find ourselves to be alien in a world upon which we were born. There are groups of people who prefer it to stay that way. Sometimes our own drug or alcohol abuse will help us negate the incessant noise of disappointment which crowds the simple thoughts of life. If we cannot do it, there are plenty of physicians with a host of pharmacological answers to ensure we have what it takes to fit in and avoid this unpleasant thought process. Particularly with regards to the struggles women face day in and day out.

As life continues to happen around each of us, we will find challenges which we did not expect and some which you simply cannot prepare for. Understanding these ancient tales contained in our lore make a world of difference in handling the hard times. Or any "times" for that matter. Not as religious doctrine; but as the kind of common sense wisdom our forefathers tried to instill in the young members of the tribe. Common sense which is short supply these days. It is still there within us. In most cases; it is occluded by all of the nonsense going on around us. Much of it we have brought upon ourselves.

But what about the man or woman who feels with every fiber of their being that there is something missing? "Surely there must be something wrong with me?" they will say to themselves. But the tragedy is that the damage has been done. Open wounds of an emotional and mental nature drive us to seek relief, like a wounded bear seeking a cave. Yet this refuge must be found in our minds and the medicines we take to make these feelings go away only serve to bandage the open wounds of our soul complex and keep us in line. We see plain as day the lies told to the entire world and we know this way of life is not for us. We believed Asatru was our answer. A way of faith which did not require us to conform. Which offered us the freedom to rebel but sadly failed to offer us the breakthrough we so desperately hoped for. This book is here to help answer some of those questions we repeatedly ask ourselves. "When will it be my time? When will I get my shot? Why did I fail when I knew I could do it?, How long do I have to feel this way?, Why do I feel so alone?, How do I access this enormous potential I feel inside, or used to feel inside?, How are these other people doing this? Am I worthless?". These questions and many more besides gnaw at our subconscious as surely as Nidhogg gnaws upon the souls of the most treacherous men. The similarity is there for a reason far beyond what we have up until now been capable of understanding. It far surpasses the idea of the Christian devil and hints at the liberation of the individual to a state of being he or she might scarcely imagine. Perhaps it is time for a long-held secret to be revealed as this world is indeed very pregnant with lies. Let's begin.

Bryan D Wilton

Friday the 13th January 2017

Better a house, though a hut it,

A man is master at home;

His heart is bleeding who needs must beg

When food he fain would have

Chapter I

The story of Exodus is a well-known tale. A grand tribe of people find a leader which leads them to a promised land. Though he himself is not fit to enter. They leave behind a life of slavery and oppression. Some will tell you that they are the ones who built the great pyramids and the masons will claim that their information dates from this era. The great stonecutters who fashioned the blocks of the pyramids and the temple of King Solomon. Trials and tribulations are their lot as they eat manna from heaven while wondering through the desert.

But the archeological evidence suggests something much different. There is evidence that the builders of the pyramids were an educated lot. Mirroring the middle class of modern society. They were well fed with talents including skilled artisans and laborers. These were a people who spent their days trading their time for someone else's dollars. Yet one of the most important stories of the old testament is of them leaving this middle-class existence behind. Why? There is a suggestion that some of them were very well off.

Because it is a journey of spiritual development. Never mind the fact that it is not "ours" per se it is still a very valid idea. The lore of the north lends itself to the development of the individual first; as a means to reinforce the powerful ideas of the tribe. There is no messianic leader to bring us heaven or hell at a later date based on a life well lived. We are living this life well and that is just the beginning of the freedom we might allow ourselves to enjoy.

As with many things in the bible much of what is written is not a literal occurrence. It is allegory. I have read similar stories and opinions concerning Ghandi and Martin Luther King Jr. A man which leads his people to a better life. Typically expressed as the concept of freedom from oppression. In some cases; the concept of oppression is clear and concise with well documented violations of the most basic of human dignities. In other cases; it is a people remembering who they are. Carl Jung pointed out the same thing occurring in the psyche of the people of Germany prior to WW2. The spirit of the tempest as Wotan blowing through the folk soul of the people. Once again, a people who were thoroughly oppressed. Inflation was so rampant that money was being used as labels on beer bottles. Jobs were scarce and the world considered them to be villains. Sure enough, someone arose to lead them to a brief, if not magnificent glory. The aftermath has taught us much. Lenin tapped into the same mentality and many more millions were killed. One type of man worked for the greater good of the people, another type of man became drunk on power. To the wise man; it becomes very clear, the whole of life is not centered around you. The insistence that it is, leads to the suffering of not only the individual but for people all around you as well. True; the scale may vary but the outcome is the same. The success of ones' efforts to lead a people to a spiritual freedom will not be successful if it focuses on outside forces. Even more so with the individual and his task of accomplishing spiritual growth. One cannot enjoy the green fields of the various heavens of the world by playing the victim.

It is easier to accomplish your goals if you find a villain. Lenin, Stalin and Hitler are but a few who have proven this. There are lots of people today who would cling to these old arguments as if they would give the individual power to achieve something. It is an ego driven attempt to justify a position. We are bombarded by them and their conspiracy theories. Knowing full well they are right yet powerless to do anything about it other than feed their ego. Scientology has performed the coup de gras upon this whole process by creating a process through which their members might consider themselves free of crime and all those against them as criminals. In this medium the insanity of a madman or the genius has been given expression to provide wealth untold of while the people languish in ways which are almost incomprehensible.

It is a mirror image of society at its worst. The members of society spend their money to live as the world expects them too. But no further. Leaders who would promote the idea that there is a way to break through the self-imposed and largely taught barriers to our success are touted to be charlatans and frauds. No one wants to believe that an average man can achieve any kind of success. Partially because we have no conception at all of what that might mean. The man who does not possess a clear image of what it means to be successful will always be drawn to the left or to the right uncertain of his ways.

You see there are all kinds of ideas and concepts in this world which seek to draw us off course. The brief summation and the examples I have used have all been sufficient to spark dialogues which fill personal libraries on the subject. It drags us away our focus from a fantastic task we have set before us just like the magazines at the checkout line of your grocery store. Right before we spend what little we may have to feed the ones we love, we may find our self caught up in the drama of the wealthy and famous, or seduced by the beautiful people who have lost weight and feel they deserve recognition for their struggle. Or the beautiful destinations around the globe we might long to see. Beaches and temples, mountains and rivers, an almost limitless expression of nature and the primal yearning to connect with it is a beautiful place to start. During the bombardment of programming and consumerism, for just a second, whenever we might see some place worth visiting, we feel that yearning which has pushed the boundaries of the world to the breaking point by our ancestors. We feel a desire to be free. But first pay for your groceries.

There comes a time for all of us who wish to be Asatru where we must grapple with disenchantment. Once the newness of the return to our ancestral faith begins to fade there is a point where we may be susceptible to the aforementioned distractions of our attention. Looking to our faith for answers we may stumble through the runes. Though lacking clarity of thought driven by a hunger to alleviate the confusion, our mindset may not be conducive to the proper understanding, much less utilization, of these powerful symbols. We are then, once again faced with the limitations of the rational and it is the last place we might wish to be. Especially after having found such a powerful indication that this may indeed be the way of life we would wish to enjoy. At some times it may feel as if a crisis of faith is upon us. Throw in a tragedy of death or great loss and it will take far more than the exuberance of youth to bear us through the hard time.

    This is the juncture where most people will take up arms as it were against the perceived wrongs of society and Christianity or monotheism. Especially if it was a predominant thought process once they adopted Asatru. They will fall back upon the ideas which angered them and offered the perception of righteous thought. Often times they have confused this sense of powerful energy for spirituality. A state of being which is easily fed. The truth of the shortcomings of the orthodoxy abound for the individual who wishes to look. The foundations of pagan beliefs in all three of the monotheistic traditions provides fuel for a self-righteous fire far too many people mistake for spiritual experience and wisdom. It is a falsehood which shackles the growth of people perhaps even worse than their adherence to monotheism which tells them to turn the other cheek and accept fate on a bended knee. The idea that everything good must originate from outside the individual is the greatest farce ever foisted upon humanity. One which has been cemented into our minds by the mortar of comfort. It is also a powerful warning of what will occur with the corruption of heathen ideals into a manmade and very powerful monopoly.

Three times in our current era, powerful polytheistic traditions have been corrupted into monotheistic machines, the effect of which we may observe in the middle east/ southwest Asia or across Europe on any given day. And in all three cases the key maintaining that control was to eliminate the power of women in this or that society.

  Being aware of these concepts is one thing; being able to utilize them to grow spiritually is quite another. Yet, as I have mentioned, there have been men and women throughout history who have illumined these ideals of spiritual stagnation and comfortable lives which have inspired great movements. These ideals and actions have been celebrated as the liberation of a people. Though I have done fine work with regards to this in all the books I've written, there is a constant stream of individuals who are dead set against an interpretation which might rob them of what they consider to be a very important source of power.

  Within the confines of the Asatru faith there might be 6000 different people with 6000 different ideas about how to interpret the lore. But it is usually deciphered in such a way that it will cause someone the least amount of pain. And just as the rivers cut the easiest way through the crust of the earth in crooked ribbons of life giving water so too will we find crooked men who lack the strength to clear away the wreckage of their lives to embrace the freedom which is mere inches away.

So, what should we do to remove these self-imposed barriers of 6000 different interpretations? Each one is the easiest interpretation with regards to any individuals' life in that moment. But just as water flows across the earth according to the easiest path, so too have we allowed the egos of men to read into the lore (or deny it completely) ideas which represent the least amount of physical discomfort with regards to growth in their lives. Most of the time, the limit of that growth is the self-satisfying idea that they are right. One man is going to have a very difficult time convincing each of these Asatruars that his way is the best. Woe be it to any woman who stands up to give a voice to their unique and often times soul crushing struggle in this world. We see the evidence of this in every online argument people may engage in.

What we have not seen is a lasting demonstration that the adoption of a certain set of ideals will lead to a commonplace success among men. But why argue about it. Let's take the same approach the Gods did. Let's change the venue and present to the assembled host a goal. It is in this manner, when everyone is feasting upon the success of our efforts that we might identify and cast aside the individuals who are still bolstering their ego. They bolster it with what they perceive as an understanding of the gods, though they are not aware that they are in fact bringing scorn upon themselves by the size of their own belly. What we must first do; is figure out exactly where we are in our life. This will require honesty which is a bane to the existence of any persons' ego.

    You see we are not only placing ourselves at odds with a society which encourages our subservient participation in the jobs which make the world go around, we are also placing ourselves in direct opposition to the teachings which represent the foundation of our own thought process. Much of the distraction of the world is there to ensure that we carry on in the same manner as everyone else. The revolutionary ideals of the great do over/end of civilization/societal downfall offers the man who subscribes to them what he hopes is the chance to begin again on his own terms and avoid tackling the issue of changing the man by changing his thoughts. That kind of change is truly painful. The realization that the ones which you have loved the most in your life have led you wrong. That they have encouraged a limited life for you because it is all they know still represents a betrayal. To realize you may have forced it upon your wife or children could be a crippling thought. The understanding of it is a deeply moving personal experience. It is also a powerful catalyst for growth. Growth which is extremely necessary for us to survive and indeed if we expect to thrive in direct opposition to much of the world.

Make no mistake, these ideas which are being reborn within the hearts and minds of men will have the same effect as the radical ideas of transformation which brought about the Renaissance. For whatever reason, every person who is reading this book, is destined to play a part in that. Else your thoughts would not have led to this point. Searching for hope and a goal while we fight the tide of society in order to enjoy a full and well-rounded life of family, love, the stories of brave men and women, and the company of good people.

These ideas of self-examination and continued growth for the individual; while they may be painful, offer us the freedom to rebuild the pillars of our being to match our new spirituality. To foster within our minds the strength to create a world we would wish to live in, one we were unaware of. To find within our emotions a full range of feeling beyond anger and loss. To discover our physical bodies still have what it takes to be strong again. By any measure of interpretation this is an awakening of the man to vast possibilities. The adoption of Asatru as a way of life extends far beyond any one aspect of our being. It is a breakthrough. An awakening which has the potential to inspire a complete man or woman. But it takes work and once all aspects have been rebuilt to serve a new purpose we may very well find that we are walking in green fields much like the Gods who return to Ithavoll after Ragnarok. To sit at golden tables and regale each other with tales of heroic struggle.

One of the key concepts we are missing is that once the change begins, such as a change in our spiritual foundation, there will inevitably follow a pattern in which the rest of our being also desires to change. After the awakening of our spirituality we may find ourselves struggling to understand the vast potential of the empowerment at our fingertips. It may well manifest itself as a restless impulse to improve ourselves so that we may be fit enough to explore the vast new spiritual horizon we now gaze upon.

The trouble begins when we conclude that we are comfortable where we are. That there is no need to change with regards to our emotional, mental or physical condition. Occasionally we will find the individual who focuses all his energies into developing a mental understanding of a spiritual journey. One will immediately see the problem when viewing it from the outside. But the individual who is in the midst of this process is oblivious. While we may spend a great deal of time taking the inventory of a myriad of individuals and their shortcomings; which is admittedly all too easy to do; we might be better focused on preventing this painful struggle by identifying it and using the tools present in the lore to work with it, instead of against it.

    This requires an intimate understanding of ourselves. Asatru has what it takes to remove the blinders of societal conformation form our eyes so that we might again see the world and know ourselves. I've always contended that the inscription over the door to the Temple of Apollo at Delphi; "Know Thyself" is a key. Julian the Apostate affirms this belief when he writes of the difference between gods and men. For what does a God understand if not himself and in that knowledge, he has used the power of it to build a world he would wish to live in. We have that same ability. It is outlined in the lore in several places. In the Song of Rig and the Lay of Hyndla, we see gods and goddesses fostering within people the idea that they do indeed have what it takes to accompany them upon their quests. Whatever that may be; it is most assuredly far better than this ego driven world men and women have created which spends some much time dangling the carrot in front of us, while at the same time hammering into our heads that we cannot do it, or that we must wait on someone else's approval.

Chapter II

The destruction of the beauty of women, their ability to love and give life has been a key component of everything which has been discussed in the previous chapters. I doubt if even faith inspires men to greater action than the love of a beautiful woman. The constant onslaught against women in this society takes many forms. It is clear in any of the ads we see on television, on the radio, in film, and in print. All of it creates doubt and a reassurance that women will be what they want to be if they would only make this or that purchase. The origins of this destruction of the sacred feminine lay squarely within the realm of monotheism and the big three Abrahamic faiths. The Spanish Inquisition, the burning of witches, the dressing down of spouses and daughters, the horrible injustices of Islam against women are just the tip of the iceberg. It is the result of men who have no confidence in themselves and dreadfully fear the pain women may cause in their hearts. A pain which no God has the power to alleviate. Pain and fear empower a male ego to take actions which might secure a foothold against the awesome power that women possess. It has resulted in the most grievous of sins. Particularly with regards to how a father should raise and care for his daughter. What "faith" would ask a man to marry off the innocence of his 9-year-old daughter? What fear would drive an entire faith to brutally remove from a young girl the future center of her pleasure zone? All she knows in that moment is that these women who are supposed to raise her and initiate her into the roles of womanhood are causing her irreparable and intense physical pain. Emotional, mental, physical and spiritual pain is forced upon the girl in the most brutal manner imaginable. It is the extreme but if we look closely we see degrees of the same effort to cripple a young girl before she even gets a chance to be a woman in this world all around us. The small-minded insecurities of men have failed to protect and cherish that which ought to be a part of the most holy.

    It is no wonder so many women have led the way back to the worshipping of the goddess.

Particularly among the tribes of Northern Europe. Yet in large part the damage has already been done. The expectations of society which are out of context with their very being have worn them out. They are tired from being in control all the time. They are exhausted from the constant complaining that they are not measuring up in some way. It is a delicate balancing act and one wrong step will get you labeled as a whore or a feminazi, or bull-dyke, spinster, control freak, anal, or any other of several monikers which point out in some way that a woman has failed or gone to the extreme to prove who and what she thinks she is. And all they are trying to do is survive in this world. Actions are taken with the sole purpose of protecting the self from further harm. Memories of emotional distress tint the image of each and every interaction until it becomes ingrained within their being. They operate on autopilot, wondering why they make the same mistakes over and over. Building emotional barriers to protect the seed of beauty each woman possesses from the corruption of society does not constitute freedom. But even the attempt to extricate oneself from the complex web a woman must navigate in todays' world results in immense loneliness and pain.

Women who have been wounded by fathers who do not have a firm grasp upon the roles and responsibilities they play in a little girl's life are everywhere. The failure of a father to properly secure in his existence the understanding of the male relationship to the female in all of its' forms is outlined in the tale of Skahdi It is also a warning to men concerning their treatment of beauty and the results it will have upon their own children. In fact; an out of balance incorporation of the feminine into the life of a man does indeed possess the potential of lethality. Once again; this is where we begin to see the poison of the Abrahamic faiths. Not possessing the courage to admit they need to figure it out, it is all too easy for them to point out a biblical role the woman must play. One which is subservient and obedient. Whose greatest achievement is that she might marry well and bear fine sons. Which is all fine and good to recognize but it also brings into view with crystal clarity that women are going to have to recover the ancient mysteries of their being largely of their own accord. But where do we start? Let's discuss the tale of Skahdi and I'll show you.

He began the story at the point where three of the Æsir, Odin and Loki and Hoenir, departed from home and were wandering over mountains and wastes, and food was hard to find. But when they came down into a certain dale, they saw a herd of oxen, took one ox, and set about cooking it. Now when they thought that it must be cooked they broke up the fire and it was not cooked. After a while had passed, they having scattered the fire a second time, and it was not cooked, they took counsel together, asking each other what it might mean. Then they heard a voice speaking in the oak up above them, declaring that he who sat there confessed he had caused the lack of virtue in the fire. They looked thither, and there sat an eagle; and it was no small one. Then the eagle said: "If ye are willing to give me my fill of the ox, then it will cook in the fire." They assented to this. Then he let himself float down from the tree and alighted by the fire, and forthwith at the very first took unto himself the two hams of the ox, and both shoulders. Then Loki was angered, snatched up a great pole, brandished it with all his strength, and drove it at the eagle's body. The eagle plunged violently at the blow and flew up, so that the pole was fast to the eagle's back, and Loki's hands to the other end of the pole. The eagle flew at such a height that Loki's feet down below knocked against stones and rock heap sand trees, and he thought his arms would be torn from his shoulders.

Here we have three powerful beings, two of whom are secure in who they are and what they are capable of, but one, one is a representation of the immature male psyche. He has something to prove. To make matters worse another powerful and immature aspect of the male psyche joins the gathering. He is resplendent in his feathers and posturing as an eagle. And the contest of egos commences. First of all, it's an argument about starting a fire. Now I don't know if you've ever been around a group of men trying to start a fire but it can be interesting. Odin and

Hoenir at this point seem to just kick back and enjoy the show. The eagle swoops in like John Wayne and shows these boys how it's done. Feeling confident about getting a fire going in front of the creator of worlds. I'm sure he was impressed. At any rate, the uninvited yet somewhat welcome guest, helps them cook the ox. Notice that this ox came from a herd so there are more of them. Loki becomes incensed that the giant has eaten ¾ of the ox and he begins to plot a way to ease his wounded ego. Instead of just grabbing another one to continue the feast which ought to be easy enough to do. Odin does possess Gungnir which always hits what it is thrown at and always kills what it hits. Loki decides to take matters into his own hands with a somewhat uninspiring course of action. If there is one thing we might be sure of, it's that Loki will kill the beings around him who makes him look bad or appear to be better than he is. Instead of improving himself he will eliminate the competition. In this particular moment; he is in front of Odin and Hoenir, he must maintain face.

A typical ego driven male response to being outdone. In this case, he decides to drive a spear into the eagles back. How many times have we each seen men and women do the exact same thing. Usually in the form of character assassination on social media or around the water cooler. The principle is the same. It is an expression of confusion and to the wise an admittance that they are jealous of something which they are not capable of. It is also a warning sign of a lazy thinking model. The next thing which happens is that the Eagle flies off and drags him thru the brambles and all that. During this dreadful clash of male egos, they begin to talk about a woman as if she is a possession to be bartered with.

He cried aloud, entreating the eagle urgently for peace; but the eagle declared that Loki should never be loosed, unless he would give him his oath to induce Idunn to come out of Ásgard with her apples. Loki assented, and being straightway loosed, went to his companions; nor for that time are any more things reported concerning their journey, until they had come home.

     These two representations of a very base mentality coupled with a masculine ego, conspire to take another mans' wife. This in itself points out a powerful misconception of the role a woman will play in the life of the masculine identity. The eagle has a daughter, who loves him dearly we might assume, But Loki and the giant Eagle have nothing but a powerful and egotistical love for themselves. The giant seeks another woman to grace his tower. It is irrelevant how he must acquire her. He knows full well he has not cultivated within himself the qualities which might match Bragi. Like most men though, knowing of the failing and having the courage to do something about it, are two very different things. They will both proceed as men will do until their doom.

     But at the appointed time Loki lured Idunn out of Ásgard into a certain wood, saying that he had found such apples as would seem to her of great virtue, and prayed that she would have her apples with her and compare them with these. Then Thjazi the giant came there in his eagle's plumage and took Idunn and flew away with her, off into Thrymheimr to his abode.

The deed is done. Through lies, trickery and deceit the masculine offers up something which isn't his to another base and simple masculine image dressed up in feathers. Feeling satisfied that he didn't need to change anything about himself to be worthy of such a mate he takes her to his castle. But such a valuable contribution to the remainder of the society is quickly noticed.

But the Æsir became straitened at the disappearance of Idunn, and speedily they became hoary and old. Then those, Æsir took counsel together, and each asked the other what had last been known of Idunn; and the last that had been seen was that she had gone out of Ásgard with Loki. Thereupon Loki was seized and brought to the Thing, and was threatened with death, or tortures; when he had become well frightened, he declared that he would seek after Idunn in Jötunheim, if Freyja would lend him the hawk's plumage which she possessed. And when he got the hawk's plumage, he flew north into Jötunheim, and came on a certain day to the home of Thjazi the giant. Thjazi had rowed out to sea, but Idunn was at home alone: Loki turned her into the shape of a nut and grasped her in his claws and flew his utmost.

Notice that it isn't just the husband who is aggrieved at the actions of Loki, but the entire society condemns the uninspired action against the divine feminine. He must also deal with another of the divine feminine to acquire a set of feathers to complete his quest. How embarrassing and completely necessary that he must deal with a mother or sister to repair the damage done. I also find it oddly reassuring that we haven't changed to such a degree that this wouldn't make sense. As soon as Thjazi has a woman at home, his trophy wife, that bastard goes fishin. And just like the relationships of today when the obnoxious individual is out fishing, the woman will leave, one way or another. I've seen it happen far too many times in this day and age.

From young professionals to your common redneck. It may not be literal fishing, it may be gaming or some very time consuming hobby or it may just be eating, sitting on the couch and watching TV. Whatever the case their minds and thinking process are a long way off. As soon as they feel like they have someone in the house who will take care of everything like their mother there is the feeling that their responsibility is handled with regards to the relationship. There is an entire chapter I'll be devoting to this problem. Right now though, we are dealing with the failing of a father to handle the concept of a woman in his life and the damage it will cause to his little girl. The story continues:

> *Now when Thjazi came home and missed Idunn, he took his eagle's plumage and flew after Loki, making a mighty rush of sound with his wings in his flight. But when the Æsir saw how the hawk flew with the nut, and where the eagle was flying, they went out below Ásgard and bore burdens of plane shavings thither. As soon as the hawk flew into the citadel, he swooped down close by the castle wall; then the Æsir*

struck fire to the plane shavings. But the eagle could not stop himself when he missed the hawk: the feathers of the eagle caught fire, and straightway his flight ceased. Then the Æsir were near at hand and slew Thjazi the giant within the Gate of the Æsir, and that slaying is exceeding famous.

    And Thjazi is destroyed by the same thing he used to secure the bargain for a woman as his trophy. Fire is a representation of an uninspired ego. Anyone who cannot begin to fathom the wisdom of this ancient tale may well be in the midst of this type of thinking. Ego masquerading as confidence. Being unable to identify such a mindset will result in subsequent failure. The second and third wife will appear more and more like a mother instead of a partner in life. Sadly; the woman who has never found a partner who will provide the domain where she might truly flourish as a woman, will accept the status as a kind of mother just dealing with it. It may well be all she has ever known. In the case of Idunn she is simply placed in a cage. A feeling many women are all too familiar with.

When we sacrificed the formalities of the man and woman making ceremonies, we failed to provide a secure footing for us to offer instruction for what was to come. We began to feel comfortable that someone else might handle it. The powerful goals of youth to be a valuable part of the tribe have been replaced with the self-seeking behaviors predominant in this world of children posing as adults. The adult men and women of the tribe understood that the children ought to be taught certain things. There was a value to the tribe in that it would continue to survive seasons and future generations would be able to prosper. When women were relegated to second class status by the church and by extension the business world and our government while others began to educate our children we lost. We lost on almost every front imaginable. The sacred teachings which had been handed down from mother to mother for generations in not only our culture of Northern Europe, but in every single indigenous culture which was forced to accept a universalist, homogenous behavior so they might better adapt to an industrialized world. The great meals our grandmothers would cook for huge families and the skill necessary to plan them were lost for the sake of expediency and the burgeoning pressures of trying to fit in with a job and the corporate world. More importantly children are not witnessing or participating in activities which foster family ties and strengthen personal development. And in the very worst cases, like Idunn; the woman simply finds herself in an alien environment much different from the one she imagined. But it is the examples of the extreme which encourage us to take a look at our life and determine if we are on track. Now that we've taken a look and scratched the surface of this story let's get to the daughter.

Now Skadi, the daughter of the giant Thjazi, took helm and birnie and all weapons of war and proceeded to Ásgard, to avenge her father. The Æsir, however, offered her reconciliation and atonement: the first article was that she should choose for herself a husband from among the Æsir and choose by the feet only, seeing no more of him. Then she saw the feet of one man, passing fair, and said: "I choose this one: in Baldr little can be loathly." But that was Njördr of Nóatún

The careless and selfish attitudes of the father have left the daughter to fend for herself. Her concept of how a man should value her may be somewhat askew, in some cases it may not be there at all. Furthermore; she has not been given a demonstration of the many faceted ideal we need to become men and women. In this society of today young men have been given no idea how to handle the delightful task of raising a daughter. His mother may be the only parent in the home. If she is dealing with the issues we have been talking about concerning her father and the men in her life it is going to be very difficult for a young man to develop a healthy and balanced attitude about himself and the women around him. For the daughter, she may well be left to determine what it is about herself which is beautiful. Which represents what it means to be feminine. She may very well be left to her own devices to determine what it is about herself which is valuable to society. The media of this day and age offers an endless litany of what that may be. While the mother struggles to understand why her femininity could not secure a future with the masculine idea she thinks she understands.

The struggle of divorce will typically last a year or so if positive work is done to deal with the emotional and mental damage. That year may well be all it takes to create unimaginable harm to a child. Sadly; it is a drug or drink which forms the acceptable manner of dealing with a loss of this type. People all around you will tell you that they aren't good enough for you as if that might make the pain unnecessary and that you ought to be capable of just getting over it. This behavior has the potential to stretch out the pain of separation to last a lifetime. Nothing short of a spiritual experience will help some of these folk, a great many of them will die in a state of confusion with the wreckage of their past stacked up around them.

Other women will take a different approach. They will become domineering with a bent to control everything around them. Snide comments which ridicule and insult become the mainstay of their vocabulary in church, at the PTA meeting, their home, where they eat and in the office. CS Lewis wrote that controlling women are the "*sort of women who live for others. You can tell the others by their hunted expression*" Every aspect of their life and the lives of those around them is planned with precise perfectionism. Never considering for a moment that this is not a virtue. Yet it is these controlling women who are held up as examples of corporate success. They are well rewarded and for the moment it may appear that everything is going as they think it should be. But the rigid and determined aspect of this type of life has a tendency to squelch the beauty within her along with her ability to express it. This is sometimes a confusing state of being, on the one hand there is the possibility of success and social acceptance, on the other hand there is a denial of a few of the aspects which most profoundly make her a woman. This confusion will sometimes be at the root of pain in a woman's life. A constant, low murmur of background noise in her thought process which suggests that this isn't really what she wants to be doing. The pain is multiplied as resentment from people all around her. And at the root of it all is the tiny little thought that maybe she wasn't woman enough.

When Skahdi picks her husband, it offers us important insight into a modern-day problem. *Then she saw the feet of one man, passing fair, and said: "I choose this one: in Baldr little can be loathly." But that was Njördr of Nóatún.* This short sentence where she must pick a man for a husband is a tale within itself. Many women will present themselves and what they believe to be the great feminine aspect of their being to a man based on a short sighted and shallow understanding of who that man is. The tale uses the idea of his feet, which I suppose is a politically correct thing to do, but today they do so because the guy is hot or some other such nonsense. When a woman bases the ideal of a man she would wish to share her life and womanhood with on just one aspect it results in pain. It usually leads to the type of miscommunication based on assumptions and results in a short-lived romance. And yet for thousands of years' women have been told they must be a compromise. As we dive into the story of Sigurd and Brunhylde we will see a tale which starts out with a woman who will not compromise. She secures a hero for herself.

    A father will do many things in his life and the daughter will pick up on what he believes to be important in his wife. She may internalize this along with constant media suggestions. This will lead to the idea that if the guy is hot, or worse, if he is a challenge to be tamed, she might be able to bring her womanly wiles to bear and prove how much of a woman she is. Confusion abounds when the guy doesn't react to her in a way which suggests he values her like her father did or did not. Very little of this is conscious decision making. It is taught behavior from watching our parents. When she finally offers to him what the young consider their vulnerable and secret passions and he continues to act in a manner which is incongruent with her expectations it is confusing and painful. But mom is at work or she may be tired. There are plenty of suggestions from our co-dependent media and loads of equally confused friends with some advice to offer. When it reaches a crisis point it may get noticed, but it is the symptom of pain which will be treated and not the behavior. It is very difficult to give something away that you do not have! The reclamation of mothers and fathers teaching our children the value of who they are is going to become a cornerstone of our faith and a bastion of hope for the society we would wish to live in.

The tale continues to offer us some insight into the confusion of expectation between men and women which we see every day. He wishes to live by the sea and she cannot stand it. She wishes to live in her father's castle (imagine that). Not being able to overcome the failings of the individuals in the relationship, the idea of being able to compromise on where to live will serve as the breaking point. Much like the lid being left up on the toilet, or the lid left off the toothpaste, or the way they eat, or they drink too much. I mean; she has brought him to her father's castle and shown him how she expects him to act, but Njördr possesses wealth untold of in those seas of his, why should he sacrifice that security? She has brought to him her greatest possession by giving of herself and her femininity, the typical expectation is that it is very valuable and he should be willing to make certain sacrifices to keep her happy. How disappointing that he would still feel his greatest security in the treasures he possesses and not within her. She still needs to know her father treasures her, like the women he has tried to keep in his castle. This is her understanding of a woman's worth to a man. That it is a treasure, a unique bauble to be cherished and fawned over. It has created an out of balance perception of worth within her very being. Though they and so many other couples we all know of today may have tried, they are working against training which has been taught to them since they were very little. Not being given the confidence to understand that love has many facets to it. You see when the mothers of our ancient tribes told these tales to young men and women they offered irreplaceable wisdom and instruction.

The instruction of men and women being the realm of women when they are young, there is a warning for egotistical young men as well:

She had this article also in her bond of reconciliation: that the Æsir must do a thing she thought they would not be able to accomplish: to make her laugh. Then Loki did this: he tied a cord to the beard of a goat, the other end being about his own genitals, and each gave way in turn, and each of the two screeched loudly; then Loki let himself fall onto Skadi's knee, and she laughed. Thereupon reconciliation was made with her on the part of the Æsir. It is so said, that Odin did this by way of atonement to Skadi: he took Thjazi's eyes and cast them up into the heavens, and made of them two stars.

It is no accident that the culprit in all of this has his very manhood touted as the butt of a joke. Make no mistake, the thought of a woman laughing at a man's private parts is one of those things which terrifies young men. Especially if their father is teaching them that women are objects to be conquered like notches on a bedpost. The online pornography business isn't much help either where every man and woman is built of magnificent proportions. Whatever the case, this particular paragraph is as much a cautionary tale to young boys as it is a demonstration of compassion and respect for a powerful female figure. And don't forget that it is Skahdi who secures the serpent above Loki's head after he finishes his egotistical self-destruction in front of the assembled Aesir. Men who cannot figure out how to recover from these very painful situations will suffer from the memory of them for a very painfully long time! Worse yet, they will force that ideal upon the other women in their lives.

Masculinity and Femininity are intricately and beautifully tied together. You really cannot have one without the other. Within each of us these concepts exist. Our inability to reconcile these harmonious and at times conflicting forces is readily apparent to every one we meet, whether we realize this or not. The ability of a man to reveal and help to cultivate the beauty of the woman he is partnered with, is the key to the success of any relationship. It is not a once and done type of deal. It is a lifelong and ever-changing, ever- growing horizon to explore. The depths of which we may never fully reach. The dignity of searching out the depths of such a love is the essence of learning, growing, and knowing what it means to become a man or a woman. But, Oh what a journey!

While the Lord of high Bilskirnir,

Whose heart no falsehood fashioned,

Swiftly strove to shatter

The seafish with his hammer

Chapter III

This book started off as a much different idea. Even now it seems whilst in between chapters; new concepts emerge. When I wrote my second book; *The Divine Feminine in Asatru* much of it was from the vantage point of a man. It is one of those confusing ideals which are ingrained holdovers from Christianity. That we would push the ideas which men hold of women onto them because we do not truly understand what they should be. I see pictures and representations of the Asynjur every single day where they are scantily clad, sporting weapons of war and appearing as tough as any man. And they may very well be. History provides us with a plethora of examples where women have had to take matters into their own hands. By every account; they are a force to be reckoned with. But in this comfortable society it is an attempt to mitigate the ideas of femininity to a level men can understand. These may be accepted by women because it represents a freedom from the mindset which vexes them so. The "you are important, but only as I allow you to be" concept.

Thinking along those lines I remember a dream I had once, years ago. I entered a room and there was a man who had committed suicide by hanging himself and there was an enchantingly beautiful woman standing in front of him. I sensed that she was somehow a partner of his, though not necessarily his wife. I used to have a bear which accompanied me in many of my dreams. This woman turned and half of her countenance was hideous to behold. She threw down some butcher's knives in front of the bear and it began to lick the blood from them. At which time she turned the knives into a shotgun and the bear hit the trigger with its claw. As I started to run, I could feel the energy leaving me and as I hit one knee, I woke up!

Now that was an odd set of thoughts to say the least! The preceding paragraphs seem to be somewhat disjointed at best. But it is the type of thinking, which, when allowed to roam, offers the type of insight necessary for the breakthrough ideas we sometimes refer to as the "ah-ha" moments. It brings me to a goddess who is much older than we typically realize and a very important idea which supports the idea of balance between the masculine and feminine ideals.

Hel has never made sense to me as outlined in the lore. We are told that she was a child of Loki and Angrboda along with the Fenris wolf and the Midgard Serpent but there is a lot of evidence that suggests a much older being. The North/South axis of older burial mounds may have been placed in such way to honor her or at the very least point the way for the dead. I've thought for a while now that Snorri has left something out of the lore to fit a narrative of his own making. One that would mirror the control that the Christian church had over its' congregations as opposed to the freedoms of the Althing.

While Hel may indeed possess those characteristics of an unappealing afterlife as we see here: *Her hall is called Sleet Cold; her dish, Hunger; Famine is her knife; Idler, her thrall; Sloven, her maidservant; Pit of Stumbling, her threshold, by which one enters; Disease, her bed; Gleaming Bale, her bed hangings. She is half blue black and half flesh color (by which she is easily recognized), and very lowering and fierce.* We learn nothing of the side of her which is beautiful. I think we will find that in this beauty we may very well find a freedom that we never expected.

    Hel is derived from a word Kolyo. Now I'm not going to get into all the semantics of the word, but it is a root word for Hail, Holy and possibly Health. Those are subjects for the scholars to debate. Valarie Wright does a pretty good job of that on her blog. Our job is to create a healthy spiritual experience so that we too might flourish with knowledge of such beauty. Once we begin to understand that, the concept of Odin granting her dominion over death over all the nine realms begins to make sense. As we see here.

    Hel he cast into Niflheim, and gave to her power over nine worlds, to apportion all abodes among those that were sent to her: that is, men dead of sickness or of old age.

I think this confusion from Snorri is a hallmark of intellectual men confronting a spiritual concept. Some people will tell you that the flesh color aspect of Hel is a truly beautiful woman and that the blue-black aspect of Hel is what lies behind her. That is the dark realms of the unknown and the veil we must cross over upon our death. It would indeed create a mysterious image. But it also brings to mind much of what we are talking about.

If the women in your life are enjoying a standard of living and freedom where they might be able to express the inner beauty of who they are and truly grow, don't you think you may have conquered one of the great mysteries of the masculine/feminine balance riddle? If your confidence in who you are is secure enough to allow the great, nurturing, passionate beings known as women to demonstrate their awesomeness without fear of jealousy or anger; as a man, you will indeed have come a long, long way towards success. Now, if you have, then which aspect of Hel do you suppose you will face when it is your turn to take up a residence in Niflheim? I would submit that I know of one resident which sets the tone for this standard; Baldur.

Frigga does an outstanding job protecting and raising her son. She goes out of her way to ensure his safety. But the one thing she hadn't counted on was the male ego. We all know how the story goes, Baldur is killed and the heart of his wife Nanna bursts with grief and she joins him in death. Once they have taken residency in the palace in Niflheim, Baldur sends back to his mother his home spun garment and many other gifts, including Draupnir to his father and finger ring for Fulla. These items represent a complete separation from the mother and sister with a powerful indication that the woman in his life, Nanna, now occupies the most prominent position. In their palace, they begin a new journey- one which will lead them to the fields of green, known as Ithavoll. Which aspect of Hel do you suppose dines within this heavenly couple? I would present to you that the most beautiful aspect of Hel is always present in the halls of Baldur's residence, as he has negotiated the mysteries of the masculine/feminine paradox and they are well on their way to a destination and life, very, very few of their old friends and family will be able to see. A fantastic place where beauty is allowed to flourish minus the shadow of contamination from ruinous behaviors and attitudes.... a place where confidence abounds.

    Death is a scary thing. No doubt about it. It is the great unknown. Only those who have actively run towards danger knowing the potential of their actions to separate themselves from everything they know or the terminally ill are qualified to tell you how frightening it can be. We would all hope to be able to face this challenge with our integrity and courage intact. Stop for just a second and consider what one thing might take the stress out of such a situation. What one concept or idea seems to lessen the fear? Beauty seems to do the trick. And apparently, it has for thousands of years.

Beauty may be a physical quality but it has served to both comfort and inspire men and women for as long we have been able to recognize it. What is it we are truly looking for in those highly romanticized walks in the woods? It is our place in the beauty of all things. For us to find ourselves figuratively wrapped in the bosom of the earth and to realize we have something of that within each of us is one of those moments which seems to make the rest of life bearable.

How often have men gone to great lengths to be recognized by a beautiful woman? The simplicity of the beauty of women is such that many images representing beautiful women are showing her at rest. At peace. A still life image to inspire and encourage. Men are beings of action. They are portrayed as being in action to convey the strength of masculinity. This is why most people will run over or distrust a passive or meek man. It is not his true nature. The deeds which might propel him to greatness seems to escape him or reside just out of reach. But that concept is for another book. While the art of men may be best characterized in art by motion, it is the simple image of beauty which stirs the imagination. A woman possesses this in spades and it may be accessed by a simple nod and a smile. To find favor with the beauty in your life is to find that part of yourself which may enjoy some rest. Some peace. To be comfortable in the chaos around us if just for a moment. To step above the cacophony of noise which permeates this modern world and threatens our sanity on many occasions. Wars have been waged, cities have been destroyed, armies have been lost while men seek to accommodate this idea of beauty in the one they love. And as we look across time and the mythologies of all the religions and faiths of the world; we see men seeking to be enveloped in the idea of love from such beauty. So much so that they would change the face of the world and attempt to move mountains to obtain it.

All a woman needs to do is smile. She knows, somewhere deep inside her, there is the potential and the desire to bring beauty to the world. The beauty of the natural world is awe inspiring indeed and has generated many works of art to honor it. But the personable beauty of a woman whose heart is secure in who she is an astounding achievement which has the power to speak of the creation of life more profoundly than anything men might dream of. How many times have we heard people talk of a woman and state that she is beautiful inside and out? That there is something about her smile or her eyes which tell us it is ok to be in her comforting presence. Grandmothers have a particularly strong hold on this most of the time. But women are a mystery. Behind her beauty lies a terrible secret, one which hampers the development of both men and women. The terrible lie most of us have been told. That we are not worth such beauty. Women especially suffer from such a tale. They will accept that it actually hurts to be beautiful.

 Beauty is an invitation to be nourished every bit as much as the babe on the mothers' breast. The loving act of breast feeding is so important it yields lifelong benefits for the child. An act of love so powerful that it biochemically changes us and speaks to us across the timespan of the rest of our lives. To see such beauty as we transition to the realm of death is such that it incorporates these ideals to aid in the stressful time of death as perceived by our ancestors. It also provides comfort to those who are still here. For those warriors left on the battlefield, unclaimed and eaten by the ravens or in the mass grave at the end of the conflict; there are beautiful women waiting for them as well. Freya takes pick of the first half and in later much romanticized tales, the Valkyries who serve Othinn gather the rest for the warriors' heaven of Valhalla. Again, we see beauty easing the transition to the great unknown and fostering bravery in those willing to die.

    Now as we may see, beauty is that element which provides our beings with what we need to embolden courage and strengthen our resolve in the face of the challenges presented by life. It really comes as no surprise that the front of Hel might be that stunningly beautiful image of a woman to embolden our terrifying transition.

The back of Hel is mysterious and dark, covered with the natural images of the earth reclaiming the material which your spirit animated. As the sun shines into the entrance of the grave mound and the back is dark and mysterious, so too is life when it operates on the principles of beauty. But in that mystery, we may find the freedom far too long denied us.

Chapter IV

In the illustration above we find an image of something along the lines of what we just discussed. The male, in this case Heimdall, bearing the fruit of his actions to Freya. She appears seated and lovely having inspired powerful action. This necklace he is handing her represents the fires of human intellect. Heimdall acquired it from Loki, who, of course stole it. One more example of him attempting to acquire something to make him greater without doing any of the work necessary to earn it. Heimdall is the whitest of the Asa, born of nine mothers and the guardian of Asgard and the Bifrost. This son of nine mothers has wrestled from the uninspired ego of the masculine a great treasure indeed. And he has given it to the Lady of the Vanir.

Let's look at this very important goddess. In just these two examples of who and what she is in the Prose Edda we will find a truly stunning outline of the problems a woman faces in our society. *Freyja is most gently born (together with Frigg): she is wedded to the man named Óđr. Their daughter is Hnoss: she is so fair, that those things*

which are fair and precious are called hnossir.
Gersemi and Hnoss are both words for treasure. They are sisters and the daughters of Freya and Odr. I find it particularly fitting that the gentle, high born goddess we know as Freya has raised her daughters to exude the same beauty to such a degree that their names are monikers for treasure itself. Isn't that what children wish to know? What girls in particular seem to strive for? To know that they are pretty and that they are valued by their mother and father. When they dress up and play with dolls they are working on establishing ideals of beauty in their own life.

They are striving to demonstrate that they are worthwhile in a parents' life. Far too often I see people who seem to be burdened by their children. The most important thing their children can do is go play somewhere or watch TV, but most importantly do not bother mom and dad. They are busy with things. They are preoccupied with something far more important than playing with the children. My sister and I heard many times that children are to be seen and not heard.

Our father went well past teaching us how to be respectful and simply told us to shut up. But he did try to spend time with us. Most fathers do. He would get down on the floor and play with his son. But I see that trying to deal with his little girl was somewhat out of his range. After all, he was kind of tired and here was a boy he could relate too, but the little girl was something of a mystery. He felt that perhaps it was just the realm of women to take care of it. He was just too tired to deal with it. That attitude carried forward even to my daughters. And his life was somewhat lessened because of it. He was conditioned himself, as he was growing up, and the job he held was exactly what he thought he was worth.

    It is a sad state of being which happens in millions of homes every single night. "I'm tired, I think I'll watch some TV and go to bed." Then we bring the stress or exhaustion of work home to our children and ignore them, they have no idea whatsoever that it is money which makes the world go around. Or worse yet and all too common, is that the parents are busy getting high or drinking and just do not want to be bothered. All they will understand is that their parents do not want anything to do with them. At the early stages of a child's development the parents are almost deities in their own right. In almost any case of abuse or neglect a child will internalize such behavior and believe that they are the cause of it. Everyone has developed a set of coping skills to handle the "bad" things which have occurred to us in our lives. They will form the basis of our interaction with everyone we meet. It is a continuation of the parents programming.

Whether or not we intend to; we give our children a message by our actions. It is clear from an early age. It does not matter if the interpretation is correct, it exists and it is the responsibility of the parent to walk a child through it. If a child makes the determination that they are going to have to fend for themselves or that they are not worth quality time. Perhaps it may come across that you were not worth loving. When we adopt that set of beliefs it is going to be very difficult to find and develop a fulfilling relationship. Children will do what they need to in order to protect their hearts. Women may feel at times that their very being draws unwanted attention with the expectation of an intimate encounter. Best to be safe and defend the heart with any kind of defense available.

The sad thing is that parents know they are doing this but seem powerless to stop their own behavior. Or even worse, justified in it. Embracing that knowledge and redirecting your purpose from the conditioning we may have received as children to one more in line with helping ourselves to become as healthy as we can be; is one of the most courageous acts a mother can take. We have a very short time in the lives of our children. If we are to raise them so that they might also be considered a treasure; let's start by ensuring, we are on solid ground ourselves.

Now we cannot play tea party and doll all of the time, but I assure you it is in your best interest to figure out the best manner in which you help your child to understand. To understand that they are precious in your eyes, that they are worth listening too, that they are loved, that they are a treasure. The world will make as many demands of you as you will allow it too. Sacrificing the future of your children to avail yourself of seemingly important things will force your children to look in other places to find a value for themselves they can live with or they will find a way to cover it all up.

I have heard it best described in this way. When a man said to his neighbor 'Why did you spend all day with your son fixing that bike? The bike shop could have taken care of it in an hour." To which the neighbor replied "Because I am building a son, not fixing a bike". The same holds true for our daughters. And the simple statement which outlines the names of Freya's daughters suggests that she is setting the example of how to do this. The high-born and noble mindset has been passed down to her daughters and their society values them.

Óðr went away on long journeys, and Freyja weeps for him, and her tears are red gold. Freyja has many names, and this is the cause thereof: that she gave herself sundry names, when she went out among unknown peoples seeking Óðr: she is called Mardöll and Hörn, Gefn, Sýr. In my duties to various organizations and personally, I have been called upon to offer counsel to a lot of people. Do you know what I hear most often from women? I briefly alluded to it in the previous chapter. It is, more often than not, a confession that she feels as if her husband has checked out. Gone fishing as it were. And much as Freya has done here, the woman will spend her time wandering through the corridors of her mind to find that one persona which attracts the attention again of the man she loves. Freya appears to be lost. Searching for someone to fill the heartache within her. Yet she does not fail in her duty to her daughters. The poignant tale of a woman struggling to find the love of her husband and raise her daughters still resonates to us from across a thousand years ago. Probably much more.

I read, years ago, this passage from a work by Kahlil Gibran, a Lebanese spiritualist: *Weeping for that which has been our delight. Our happiness or joy is contained within the very containers within us which have been carved out by our sorrow. Yet still the process will continue. Until now we have been unaware that we might possess any manner of control over this artificial encumberment.* And I can think of no better words to describe the opportunity the pain of a woman may provide. For it is an awakening to come upon this realization. Every woman has a choice now as to whether the containers which are designed to hold a happy spirituality within her are full of tears or that joy we are worthy of.

Perhaps there was a lacking sense of self which prompted her to associate with the dwarves. A fine representation of lesser men who only value her for one thing. Many women have made this same mistake. Lowering their standards to accommodate a faulty sense of self-worth. They will "treat" themselves to this or that self-indulgent behavior in any number of venues. Shopping, eating, drinking, men or they may set about to control everything around them. It is all a defensive posture designed to afford the best protection available for the heart of a woman. On occasion these indulgent behaviors become traps far worse than the condition they were meant to avoid. Instead of offering the hoped-for protection; after years of defensive posturing, all it serves to do is separate a woman from her heart and the very essence of her femininity.

But somewhere along the way, Freya remembers that she is a goddess. That there is something truly divine which resides within her and affects the entirety of the nine realms. For the women of today her acceptance and development of the divine self represents a freedom from the abuse the world is so ready to heap upon them. But it starts very simply. No one finds themselves in these situations overnight and they cannot resolve the complexity of such situations in one night. Usually, it is a simple decision which begins the entire process. A decision to follow the example of Freya and employ a little bit of faith.

From her loss, Freya recovers and she understands that she is worth possessing the necklace known as the Brisingamen. The fires of the human intellect. Fires which are the illumination for science, art, poetry and all manner of invention as well as spiritual and emotional development. Then she is again known as the Lady of the Vanir. *Freyja had the necklace Brísingamen. She is also called Lady of the Vanir.*

We look at this simple tale and we discover the elegance of the woman who has struggled but not forgotten her worth. It has not stopped her from becoming the very personification of beauty. She has shed the self-imposed burden of shame based on the actions of others. To have a little cry over all that has seemingly been lost and then to stand again in the glorious radiance as a goddess is something which every woman in Asatru has the chance to obtain. After a powerful awakening there follows an empowerment. In some ways; the future of everything we hold dear depends upon this awakening of women.

> But Freyja is the most renowned of the goddesses; she has in heaven the dwelling called Fólkvangr, and wheresoever she rides to the strife, she has one half of the kill, and Odin half, as is here said:
>
> Fólkvangr 't is called, | where Freyja rules
>
> Degrees of seats in the hall;
>
> Half the kill | she keepeth each day,
>
> And half Odin hath.
>
> Her hall Sessrúmnir is great and fair. When she goes forth, she drives her cats and sits in a chariot; she is most conformable to man's prayers, and from her name comes the name of honor, Frú, by which noblewomen are called. Songs of love are well pleasing to her; it is good to call on her for furtherance in love."

Here we see the culmination of Freya's acceptance of her role. She is a benefit to everyone. The living and the dead and her very name is a noble title bestowed upon women. Love becomes a hobby of hers and the world benefits from it. She appears to be that good friend which every woman should have in their life. Freya does not hide as so many women do with activities. Nor does she appear to fear rejection. She is no longer afraid and refuses to let that divine aspect of herself be diminished by men or women who are still afraid. Her wounds of the heart have not crippled her. We should hope that all women might find the strength of example to follow suit. In fact; she takes the opposite approach and does her best to foster within people the idea of love. All women possess such power. From the innocent smile of a little girl to the kind nod of a wise grandmother or the loving smile of a man's wife and the praise of anyone's mother, this is all it takes to change to world for whoever may be on the receiving end of it. And so it would seem that the fires of inspiration reside exactly where they should.

There is another tale where Freya takes a personal interest in one of her champions. The Hyndluljoth. This short excerpt provides some

very important insights into masculine and feminine relations.

Freyja spake:
1. "Maiden, awake! | wake thee, my friend,
My sister Hyndla, | in thy hollow cave!
Already comes darkness, | and ride must we
To Valhall to seek | the sacred hall.

2. "The favor of Heerfather | seek we to find,
To his followers gold | he gladly gives;
To Hermoth gave he | helm and mail-coat,
And to Sigmund he gave | a sword as gift.

3. "Triumph to some, | and treasure to others,
To many wisdom | and skill in words,
Fair winds to the sailor, | to the singer his art,
And a manly heart | to many a hero.

4. "Thor shall I honor, | and this shall I ask,
That his favor true | mayst thou ever find;

Though little the brides | of the giants he loves.

5. "From the stall now | one of thy wolves lead forth,
And along with my boar | shalt thou let him run;
For slow my boar goes | on the road of the gods,
And I would not weary | my worthy steed."

Hyndla spake:
6. "Falsely thou askest me, | Freyja, to go,
For so in the glance | of thine eyes I see;

On the way of the slain | thy lover goes with thee.
Ottar the young, | the son of Instein."

Freyja spake:
7. "Wild dreams, methinks, | are thine when thou sayest
My lover is with me | on the way of the slain;
There shines the boar | with bristles of gold,
Hildisvini, | he who was made
By Dain and Nabbi, | the cunning dwarfs.

8. "Now let us down | from our saddles leap,
And talk of the race | of the heroes twain;
The men who were born | of the gods above,

9. "A wager have made | in the foreign metal
    Ottar the young | and Angantyr;

We must guard, for the hero | young to have,
His father's wealth, | the fruits of his race.

10. "For me a shrine | of stones he made—,
    And now to glass | the rock has grown—;
    Oft with the blood | of beasts was it red;
    In the goddesses ever | did Ottar trust.

11. "Tell to me now | the ancient names,
    And the races of all | that were born of old:
Who are of the Skjoldungs, | who of the Skilfings,
    Who of the Othlings, | who of the Ylfings,
Who are the free-born, | who are the high-born,
The noblest of men | that in Mithgarth dwell?"

    How many people have taken notice that it is two women, one of whom is very simple and lives in a cave; while the other, Freya, is of the most noble and high born, who provides support and instruction of heritage and heraldry. They are the escort of the masculine to an ascendency of sorts. There is a parallel between a boy becoming a man and man entering the hereafter. Indeed; a man is on a journey throughout his life and it will be women of one sort or another who guide this journey. When a man fails to recognize the guide, and misinterprets the attention as desire, he is deviating from the path and he will become lost for a moment or a lifetime. There is also a great deal of confusion whereby a boy or man expects the feminine to validate his masculinity. They are merely pointing the way. Providing the details as it were. The making of the man occurs in the presence of other men and creates the environment where women may fulfill these roles. It is also very difficult for women of today to understand their role as well. The Greeks and the Japanese both had women whose sole purpose was to provide intelligent conversation and companionship without the sexual aspect involved whatsoever. This tale is a reminder of that. Though the simple and rejected woman in the cave more closely resembles the women of today in that they cannot tell the difference. They have been taught that the value of their being is something other than what they are. There are as many interpretations of that last sentence as there are women who read this book.

It is no accident that these women seek each other out to handle the duty of a man on the journey to who he is supposed to become. One of whom has beauty radiating from her very being, while the other has no one at all seeking to uncover the beauty of who she is. Yet her intelligence and her knowledge of Ottars' past is above reproach. Hyndla is a woman who has withered into the old crone as it were and now lives in a cave. Completely rejected by the world and alone. But it takes both of them to bring out the best in the man.

Many women who have suffered rejection will at times feel the same way. There is almost a visible light within which seems to be extinguished. Or at least covered up for safe keeping. But as soon as someone shows an interest in their being, if they can withstand the barbs and mean comments, they will be rewarded with a fantastic experience of wisdom and will sometimes witness a blossoming of sorts.

    The hailing of Hyndla as "sister" is an interesting thing in itself. How many times have we seen a woman and thought to ourselves "I don't want to be associated with that.". When we see noble and high born Freya hail a giantess as a sister it is a lesson. Every woman has something to offer to the processes of society and we are reminded of it at almost every turn of the page within our lore. Though our understanding of it has been tainted by generations of being taught that women are evil. From fallen Eve to the lesson of Pandoras box and the burning of the witches at the stake to today's treatment of women in the Muslim world. The hyper-aggressive controlling attitude of todays feminist "role models" we are not finding the proper role of women which is be celebrated and fostered into something which is to be embraced as a cornerstone of our societal foundations. There is the insinuation from these role models that maybe you shouldn't even try to be pretty anymore. When a woman learns, and takes that to heart, there is at some level the belief that she doesn't have anything to offer. That her place as a second-class citizen is just something she is going to have to deal with in her life. That perhaps her heart isn't enough to be worthwhile in this world. It will sometimes express itself through the ego. How much easier is it to point out a woman who may live a somewhat different life. Do you really want to be associated with a woman like that?

    Freya has been through the wringer herself. The loss of the masculine in her life has caused her such pain that the world is littered with her tears. The legend of the amber found all along the coast of the Baltic Sea, which is so valued, is that they are the tears of Freya. But I digress. The point is that one woman is lifting up and supporting another woman no matter her situation. This action has benefits for all of society and has done so since long before we were able to write it down.

I can clearly picture in my mind the elder women of ancient tribes reminding the little girls and boys to take of care of each other. With the same grand stories we are reading today. We see it in our lives when grandchildren sit upon the laps of their grandmas and listen intently to the stories of loving women with caring hands. We can all be sure that grandmas have had to deal with things in their lives which have caused them immense pain. Yet when the love of a young child offers itself to such a woman, the inner beauty arises to the occasion and we see that just like Hyndla being called out of the cave great things begin emerge.

Chapter V

The story of Skadhi resonates with so many women, and will even moreso with this little book because her actions touch upon the ideas of empowerment women may be searching when they discover there is no man around to protect them. The same thing might be said for Freya. Her search for the powerful masculine to provide the complimentary opposing force in her world causes he immense pain. But with the examples I have used so far and the identification of just a fraction of the pain and problem women deal with, we have only scratched the surface.

How many women do you know who have been assaulted in some way? Almost every woman I know has internalized pain of this type in some way. How many of those women internalize that pain because of the feeling deep within them that their fathers indicated "you are a girl but not one who is pretty enough to get my attention."? This thinking process may bear fruit as a constant thought which suggests "you are a disappointment". For some women, the simple act of reading these words will bring tears to their eyes. A typical and all too common culmination of such thinking is the disastrous marriage to a man based upon an understanding of just one aspect of him. The idea of deserving it (the violence or denigration of a woman in the relationship) or being at fault for it becomes accepted within the mind of many women and the light within them shines a little less brightly. Something like %60 of marriages will fail in the US. Their shame buried deep within them and seemingly proof that their father or mother may have been right all along. That they may not be worthy of the love everyone is so fond of reading about or watching on the television and film. Women are living with this pain every day.

      When you take into consideration the absolute onslaught against women at every turn within this world we live in it can be somewhat disheartening. It has gone on for centuries in every corner of the globe. Except within the tribes of northern Europe. Where women had the right to kick their husbands out, to be held in high regard and be leaders. In our oldest texts concerning the heathens of Germania we are told that they were revered in many instances as conduits to the divine. Judaism, Hinduism, Islam, Christianity have all waged unending wars against the beauty and life bearing divinity of women. Various governments and political ideals have been every bit as crushing as dogmatic belief systems. And our world pays for it every day.

    Though I have touched upon just a few of the many and complex solutions women may find acceptable in this society as a manner to deal with the issues, I have not provided a suggestion as to how you might overcome them or even where one might look in this faith to find the hope necessary to do so. There are a couple of places within the lore which touch on this. Freya, we see, rises to the occasion despite the very worst of circumstances and personal abuse. Primarily because she believes in herself. But the strength of this faith and way of life along with the freedom which women are deserving is outlined in two stories I can think of off the top of my head. Thor and Sif along with Frey and Gerhdr. As men; we have failed, en masse, to demand the best for the women in our life much less create an environment where they may undertake the painful process of reclaiming an ideal. But where do we start?

Simply knowing about a complex and troublesome thinking process or becoming aware of immense pain buried very deep may be overwhelming. Lots of women seek professional or faith based counseling. They will turn to "mother's little helper" as well. The ideas of awakening and empowerment seems to be somewhat far off. Maybe even so far off they aren't worth reaching for. It is also at odds with the idea of hiding that within you which seems most vulnerable. Your heart. Your heart is also where you should start. This will require courage and honesty to stand against the teachings which have been foisted upon you.

Where does a woman find the courage to once again proudly display the alluring beauty which has made so many of them so unforgettable? It will start with those women who are also on this path. Sisters, much as Freya has done with Hyndla, but also in the safety of the great palaces which have been built to ensure they have what it takes to be as great as they can be. That they can do so in safety because of the great warriors which inhabit Asgard alongside them. The masculine has gone to great lengths to create a world where women may continue to excel in everything they do. The future of their world depends upon it. Just consider what happens when even one of them is compromised as in the case of Idunn. In the ancient past the entire tribe had a say when a man worked some kind of ill against a woman. Women had no qualms in insisting that they do so. The cries of women whose men were on the verge of defeat had what it took to turn the tides of war. Such was the seriousness with which men took this charge. Thor is no exception such as in the tale of how Sif came by her golden hair.

"Why is gold called Sif's Hair? Loki Laufeyarson, for mischief's sake, cut off all Sif's hair.

But when Thor learned of this, he seized Loki, and would have broken every bone in him, had he not sworn to get the Black Elves to make Sif hair of gold, such that it would grow like other hair.

    This is an assault upon the divine feminine by the uninspired human ego. To rob a woman of her beauty, her hair being just one of the outward displays. To steal that from a woman in this literary sense has much darker connotations. To do so against the wife of the warder of men is reminiscent of what is happening in todays' world. Our women are assaulted by similar ideas on a daily basis. From our daughters and mothers to our sisters and wives. There are any number of movements and ideas, religions and charlatans would seek to convince them that there is no need to display their beauty or their confidence. That it is something which they should be ashamed of or kept covered up. Worst of all are the men who would subscribe to these ideas and consider the conquest of women a worthy enterprise. This attitude of unwanted expectation of intimacy with every female a man like this may meet has a way of reminding a woman that their beauty serves only to create problems. Others consider these acts to be a valid part of warfare and revenge. Suffice it to say the action of Loki against Sif is a violation similar to any of these ideas and ones which are much worse. It is considered a violation of the sanctity of the entire tribe.

In the history of the treatment of women around the world there has been a distinct lack of nobility involved. Physical abuse and rapes are far more common around the world than we might any of us wish to believe. There may well be hundreds of thousands of women and girls consigned to sexual slavery. Much like Thor, it is the duty of men to put an end to this. But the debt for this violation is owed to all of society.

After that, Loki went to those dwarves who are called Ívaldi's Sons; and they made the hair, and Skídbladnir also, and the spear which became Odin's possession, and was called Gungnir. Then Loki

wagered his head with the dwarf called Brokkr that
Brokkr's brother Sindri could not make three other
precious things equal in virtue to these. Now when they
came to the smithy, Sindri laid a pigskin in the hearth
and bade Brokkr blow, and did not cease work until he
took out of the hearth that which he had laid therein.
But when he went out of the smithy, while the other
dwarf was blowing, straightway a fly settled upon his
hand and stung: yet he blew on as before, until the
smith took the work out of the hearth; and it was a
boar, with mane and bristles of gold. Next, he laid gold
in the hearth and bade Brokkr blow and cease not from
his blast until he should return. He went out; but again
the fly came and settled on Brokkr's neck, and bit now
half again as hard as before; yet he blew even until the
smith took from the hearth that gold ring which is
called Draupnir. Then Sindri laid iron in the hearth
and bade him blow, saying that it would be spoiled if
the blast failed. Straightway the fly settled between
Brokkr's eyes and stung his eyelid, but when the blood
fell into his eyes so that he could not see, then he
clutched at it with his hand as swiftly as he could,
while the bellows grew flat, and he swept the fly from

him. Then the smith came thither and said that it had come near to spoiling all that was in the hearth. Then he took from the forge a hammer, put all the precious works into the hands of Brokkr his brother, and bade him go with them to Ásgard and claim the wager.

Even the story of the creation of these fine gifts is tainted with how far men will go to avoid feeling the shame of their crimes. All of these gifts will fail their owners during the Ragnarok. Much like the incomplete set of tools men are given, they find them woefully inadequate when the various crisis of life rear their ugly heads. Midlife being particularly common and it will be women who are blamed and women who become the victims of such shortsighted ego boosting attitudes.

"Now when he and Loki brought forward the precious gifts, the Æsir sat down in the seats of judgment; and that verdict was to prevail which Odin, Thor, and Freyr should render. Then Loki gave Odin the spear Gungnir, and to Thor the hair which Sif was to have, and Skídbladnir to Freyr, and told the virtues

of all these things: that the spear would never stop in its thrust; the hair would grow to the flesh as soon as it came upon Sif's head; and Skídbladnir would have a favoring breeze as soon as the sail was raised, in whatsoever direction it might go, but could be folded together like a napkin and be kept in Freyr's pouch if he so desired.

Three gods sit in judgement of the shyld Loki offers to amend the wrong he has wrought. A spear which never misses and always kills wait it hits. Gungnir has become so holy that oaths were sworn upon it. To Thor, Loki has offered the gift of golden hair to replace that which he has stolen. That Sif might appear more glorious and fantastic than ever. One cannot help but to think that she is still marred by the experience especially now that everyone knows how she obtained such a fantastic gift. That will be the first thought of many women. But in this day and age when the temptation to hide and feel ashamed is commonplace we should also consider that it was her husband who stepped up to right the wrong and do his best to support his wife. Isn't that what most women want, to feel as if they are still worthy, still beautiful in their partner's eyes. How many women carry within them the thought that "if you really knew all about me, you wouldn't love me.". Thor's actions are a refutation of that thought process. He stands up for his wife. It is in this thought process and ensuing action that men and women might enjoy smooth sailing and a favorable breeze. The notion that Frey, the god who has never made a maiden cry, is in possession of such a ship seem to be most appropriate.

Then Brokkr brought forward his gifts: he gave to Odin the ring, saying that eight rings of the same weight would drop from it every ninth night; to Freyr he gave the boar, saying that it could run through air and water better than any horse, and it could never become so dark with night or gloom of the Murky Regions that there should not be sufficient light where he went, such was the glow from its mane and bristles. Then he gave the hammer to Thor, and said that Thor might smite as hard as he desired, whatsoever might be before him, and the hammer would not fail; and if he threw it at anything, it would never miss, and never fly so far as not to return to his hand; and if be desired, he might keep it in his sack, it was so small; but indeed it was a flaw in the hammer that the fore shaft was somewhat short.

Now we witness the giving of three more great and powerful gifts. Odin is given a ring which drops eight more of its kind every ninth night. As a chieftain, it is his duty to hand out arm rings to his warriors. Every nine nights is reminiscent of the nine months a woman will carry a child. The idea that the tribe is so strong that every nine days, months or years there are eight new men to be made into warriors by the gifting of these rings suggests the making of a powerful tribe. This is repeated in the golden boar, a very fertile creature which breeds prodigiously. When such a gift is given to a god of abundance and fertility it suggests that the tribe is strong enough to support such growth. That it is a light in dark places and may travel the realms over sea or air faster than any horse seems to ensure that these new warriors will seemingly always know their way. Finally, we come to Mjolnir. The great hammer which may destroy and create, which sanctifies the burial ship of Baldr and provides a great defense for the tribe as mighty as Gungnir.

    The message is clear. When Thor stands to the defense of his wife, when the society rallies to reinforce the position of women within it. The tribe or society is empowered beyond what we might imagine. We are living in a time which is the direct opposite of such an ideal. We live in trepidation of the collapse of our society by outside forces and depend upon other outside forces to save us. When what we should have been doing all along is taking care of what is in our own homes. When I suggest that the resurgence of the importance of women in our world is a cornerstone of the foundation of our society and the continuance of our faith; this is where I get that idea. This is how we secure our existence.

Chapter VI

What about the woman who understands who and what she is? What about the woman who has enjoyed the love and protection of a father who has built a powerful residence where a girl might grow to be a woman in safety. Whose beauty is stunning even from halfway around the world. This type of woman presents a challenge to the fairest of gods and men. The lord of Alfheim and the god who has never caused a woman to cry. Perhaps her actions might empower women by example. Let's peruse the story of Frey and Gerth.

Freyr, the son of Njorth, had sat one day in Hlithskjolf, and looked over all the worlds. He looked into Jotunheim, and saw there a fair maiden, as she went from her father's house to her bower. Forthwith he felt a mighty love-sickness. Skirnir was the name of Freyr's servant; Njorth bade him ask speech of Freyr. He said:

1. "Go now, Skirnir! | and seek to gain
Speech from my son;

*And answer to win, | for whom the wise one
Is mightily moved."*

Skirnir spake:
*2. "Ill words do I now | await from thy son,
If I seek to get speech with him,
And answer to win, | for whom the wise one
Is mightily moved."*

Skirnir spake:
*3. "Speak prithee, Freyr, | foremost of the gods,
For now I fain would know;
Why sittest thou here | in the wide halls,
Days long, my prince, alone?"*

Freyr spake:
*4. "How shall I tell thee, | thou hero young,
Of all my grief so great?
Though every day | the elfbeam dawns,
It lights my longing never."*

Skirnir spake:
*5. "Thy longings, methinks, | are not so large
That thou mayst not tell them to me;*

*Since in days of yore | we were young together,
We two might each other trust."*

      We first find a wise god who has drifted off the path somewhat and come across something for which he was not prepared. Many men do. And it is among men that they will determine a course of action. Not as barbarous heathens. But with wisdom and confidence bred of strength. It is a fine thing to see a father pay attention to his son and a finer thing to see men who may confide in one another with trust. These are not men who have decided that they need a woman to validate their existence or their manliness. They already have a grasp upon this. This is the real deal. Yet we may sense that the reluctance to dive into something of this nature. A relationship which I believe he knows will require more himself than just the cordial compromise of people sharing the same space. Knowing that, even amongst such beings as the gods, there may still be the manifestation of a man's deepest fear. That is the fear of rejection.

So his father Njorth and his longtime friend Skirnir come to his support.

Freyr spake:
6. "From Gymir's house | I beheld go forth
A maiden dear to me;
Her arms glittered, | and from their gleam
Shone all the sea and sky.

7. "To me more dear | than in days of old
Was ever maiden to man;
But no one of gods | or elves will grant
That we both together should be."

      To behold a woman who glitters and gleams so that it shines throughout the sky and the sea is quite a compliment. It is also an alien concept to a god who is rooted squarely with the natural and powerful feeling of the earth. Not being familiar with these realms her beauty dominates, he appears to be relying on someone else to give him permission which would allow them to be together. There's that old masculine idea. I may not be worthy enough to do this but I really want it so I'll ask someone to give her to me. But it doesn't work. So Skirnir agrees to be a messenger for him. What follows is the outfitting of a man to handle an arduous journey. Most of it I will use in a book about men someday.

Skirnir spake:
18. "I am not of the elves, | nor the offspring of gods,
Nor of the wise Wanes;
Though I came alone | through the leaping flame
Thus to behold thy home.

Notice that this man passes thru the flames in much the same way Sigurd does to approach Brunnhylde. A boy becoming a man.

19. "Eleven apples, | all of gold,
Here will I give thee, Gerth,
To buy thy troth | that Freyr shall be
Deemed to be dearest to you."

Gerth spake:
20. "I will not take | at any man's wish

These eleven apples ever;
Nor shall Freyr and I | one dwelling find
So long as we two live."

      Strike one for the suitor. These apples of gold offer immortality. The idea that this suitor might offer her beauty for the rest of her life. That she will be appealing to the man who loves her for the rest of their days. Isn't that what most woman want? To know that their man will always desire them? Gerdhr's mindset is the complete opposite of what so many women are dealing with today. She is not plagued with ideas that the sometimes terrible situations which befall her are her fault. She even makes a statement that she fears she is allowing her brothers killer in the house. But she does not internalize this turn of events as something which she has brought about. This offer of eleven golden apples has no appeal to a woman who does not need a man to let her know she is beautiful. This is a woman who has a handle on that and is secure in her radiance. She is not concerned with how anyone feels about her one way or another. She has a handle on her personal worth and power.

Skirnir spake:
21. "Then do I bring thee | the ring that was burned

Of old with Othin's son;
From it do eight | of like weight fall
On every ninth night."

Gerth spake:
22. "The ring I wish not, | though burned it was
Of old with Othin's son;
In Gymir's home | is no lack of gold
In the wealth my father wields."

Strike two and first base is looking pretty far away. This woman has no interest in the short-sighted belief that a man's wealth will make him a worthy husband. Far from it. It is another case of a man offering a woman but one aspect of himself and she knows it. She grew up with abundance and considers herself to be a part of that. But what about the woman who has not?

Who might have grown up in abject poverty or lived from paycheck to paycheck like most people. Perhaps she has always felt her family did not truly value her. What is she worth? Would such an offer be enough to try and stop the feelings of aloneness as we watch the rest of the world live in opulence? In this day and age it most likely would be. Isn't that what we've all seen in the movies? When the handsome prince finds the beauty in the most unlikely of places and they live happily ever after. From the time little girls are old enough to understand they, are taught that there is someone who will sweep them off of their feet and they will live happily ever after. Money is how you determine that future success. Isn't it? While it may be an indicator of a man's ability to negotiate the world of business and finance; it is no reassurance that he will value your heart. And that is what must happen before any kind of fairy tale ending is to occur. You've got to begin to love your own heart and recognize it as the treasure it is. One which has the ability to change the world.

Skirnir spake:
23. "Seest thou, maiden, | this keen, bright sword
That I hold here in my hand?
Thy head from thy neck | shall I straightway hew,
If thou wilt not do my will."

Gerth spake:
24. "For no man's sake | will I ever suffer
To be thus moved by might;
But gladly, methinks, | will Gymir seek
To fight if he finds thee here."

Skirnir spake:
25. "Seest thou, maiden, | this keen, bright sword
That I hold here in my hand?

Before its blade the | old giant bends—,
Thy father is doomed to die.

Here we have the great phallic symbol of masculinity, the sword, being waved around like it's impressive or something. It's a standard tactic. It's also one of those abusive tactics we have all seen from women who are in such relationships.

The threat of abuse to Gerdhr and her family has kept many women in almost unbearable situations. For a woman such as Gerdhr it holds no sway. We have a mindset demonstrated in her which suggests she knows what she is worth and she is equally sure her father does as well.

26. "I strike thee, maid, | with my magic staff,
To tame thee to work my will;
There shalt thou go | where never again
The sons of men shall see thee.

27. "On the eagle's hill | shalt thou ever sit,
And gaze on the gates of Hel;
More loathsome to thee | than the light-hued snake
To men, shall thy meat become.

28. "Fearful to see, | if thou comest forth,
Hrimnir will stand and stare,
(Men will marvel at thee;)

More famed shalt thou grow | than the watchman of the gods!
Peer forth, then, from thy prison,

29. "Rage and longing, | fetters and wrath,
Tears and torment are thine;
Where thou sittest down | my doom is on thee
Of heavy heart
And double dole.

30. "In the giants' home | shall vile things harm thee
Each day with evil deeds;
Grief shalt thou get | instead of gladness,
And sorrow to suffer with tears.

31. "With three-headed giants | thou shalt dwell ever,
Or never know a husband;
(Let longing grip thee, | let wasting waste thee,—)

Be like to the thistle | that in the loft
Was cast and there was crushed.

32. "I go to the wood, | and to the wet forest,
To win a magic wand;

I won a magic wand.

33. "Othin grows angry, | angered is the best of the gods,

Freyr shall be thy foe,
Most evil maid, | who the magic wrath
Of gods hast got for thyself.

34. "Give heed, frost-rulers, | hear it, giants.
Sons of Suttung,
And gods, ye too,
How I forbid | and how I ban
The meeting of men with the maid,
(The joy of men with the maid.)

35. "Hrimgrimnir is he, | the giant who shall have thee
In the depth by the doors of Hel;
To the frost-giants' halls | each day shalt thou fare,
Crawling and craving in vain,
(Crawling and having no hope.)

36. "Base wretches there | by the root of the tree
Will hold for thee horns of filth;
A fairer drink | shalt thou never find,
Maid, to meet thy wish,
(Maid, to meet my wish.)

37. *"I write thee a charm | and three runes therewith,
Longing and madness and lust;
But what I have writ | I may yet unwrite
If I find a need therefor."*

And there it is. In these stanzas he gives pause for her to consider. These are the deepest fears all women possess. That they will be alone, that the beauty of youth will fade and they will no longer be in charge of their lives, that vile men will abuse them. These thoughts and many more besides have plagues women for centuries and entire religions have been built upon it. The fear that a woman may have to settle for someone who does not quite measure up to a dream long held since she was a girl. Is this a common sense argument? Is it really a play on everything a woman fears? That she will no longer find the ability to create desire in the man she might love and that he will reject her. But Frey has made a powerful sacrifice we may have forgotten about. He has given that powerful phallic symbol of the sword to another man. He has set aside the symbol of egotistical thinking among men to form a fine partnership with a complementing opposing force. And he is not one less bit the man for it, while Gerdhr assumes a place in the pantheon of Asgard. A fine compromise for a beautiful couple. And when it comes time for the world to end in the Ragnarok, Frey goes forth to fight the greatest threat of them all. He will face the fire which consumes the world to protect that which he loves with the horn of a stag. I can think of no thing which has a more powerful and lovely promise to it. For a woman to conquer those fears which plague her and to take a position next to a man who will do anything to protect the beauty he sees within her. And so; the happy ending of the story is at hand.

Gerth spake:
38. "Find welcome rather, | and with it take
The frost-cup filled with mead;
Though I did not believe | that I should so love
Ever one of the Wanes."

Skirnir spake:
39. "My tidings all | must I truly learn

Ere homeward hence I ride:
How soon thou wilt | with the mighty son
Of Njorth a meeting make."

Gerth spake:
40. Barri there is, | which we both know well,
A forest fair and still;
And nine nights hence | to the son of Njorth
Will Gerth there grant delight."

Then Skirnir rode home. Freyr stood without, and spoke to him, and asked for tidings:

41. "Tell me, Skimir, | ere thou take off the saddle,
Or farest forward a step:
What hast thou done | in the giants' dwelling
To make glad thee or me?"

Skirnir spoke:
42. "Barri there is, | which we both know well,
A forest fair and still;
And nine nights hence | to the son of Njorth
Will Gerth there grant delight."

Freyr spake:
43. "Long is one night, | longer are two;
How then shall I bear three?
Often to me | has a month seemed less
Than now half a night of desire."

If this were the only place where one finds the idea of a woman standing her ground until a suitable man arrives we might dismiss it as an idea which wasn't held as important. An idea which people just considered a fairy tale. But there is another one which is just as important. And that is the tale of Sigurd and Brunnhylde.

It is a wonderful tale of a young man who forges a sword with the help of the gods. His youth is spent in the developing of a man. The great sword he has forged is, once again, a representation of manhood and he uses it to slay the dragon. All men must go through an initiation of this sort. But that is a chapter for a much different book. For the purposes of this book we will begin with the fires the young man must walk through to prove his worth to a woman. He is not waiting on the woman to allow him to be a man. He has already proven it. But more importantly the magnificent woman he finds when he does cross the flames was not waiting on a man to tell her how great of a woman she is. She was well aware of this fact and was fully comfortable waiting on the right man to present himself as a worthy mate.

Sigurth rode up on Hindarfjoll and

turned southward toward the land of

the Franks. On the mountain he saw a

great light, as if fire were burning, and

the glow reached up to heaven. And

when he came thither, there stood a

tower of shields, and above it was a

banner. Sigurth went into the shieldtower,

and saw that a man lay there

sleeping with all his war-weapons. First he took the helm from his head, and then he saw that it was a woman. The mail-coat was as fast as if it had grown to the flesh. Then he cut the mail-coat from the head-opening downward, and out to both the arm-holes. Then he took the mail-coat from her, and she awoke, and sat up and saw Sigurth, and said:

      Waiting so long that the protection forged to shield her from the harms of this world had become encrusted to her like a second skin. How many women can tell these days where the beauty of her heart ends and the protection she has built begins. While we may be tempted to believe it is a damsel in distress situation it may also be viewed as the powerful reunion of complementing, competing forces. A wild and untamable idea which has the ability to empower both parties to ascend to success far beyond what they may have envisioned in their youth.

1. "What bit through the byrnie? | how

was broken my sleep?

Who made me free | of the fetters pale?"

He answered:

"Sigmund's son, | with Sigurth's

sword,

That late with flesh | hath fed the

ravens."

Sigurth sat beside her and asked her

name. She took a horn full of mead and

gave him a memory-draught.

2. "Hail, day! | Hail, sons of day!

And night and her daughter now!

Look on us here | with loving eyes,

That waiting we victory win.

3. "Hail to the gods! | Ye goddesses,

hail,

And all the generous earth!

Give to us wisdom | and goodly speech,

And healing hands, life-long.

    The idea of healing hands and faith in the gods (whatever your belief) is only strengthened by this union. Of course we all know that lesser people upon seeing the potential danger to the status quo do their best to destroy it all. And this is the way it has been for millennia. Lesser men and women have waged war upon the idea of empowered women. Yet here we are, looking at these tales of our ancient past and finding the encouragement to rid ourselves of the pain old wounds have caused us. There is no magical spell or divine intervention which will strike us and create a whole and complete person. But there is the constant, gentle reminder that these gods and ancestors are a part of us and that we do have what it takes to tackle these enormous challenges. They are encouraging us to breathe deeply and be at peace with the love and confidence which is our birthright.

Made in the USA
Middletown, DE
14 March 2025